The Catechesis of the Good Shepherd in a Parish Setting

REVISED EDITION

Tina Lillig

Revised by Mary Mirrione

All quotations from Scripture are taken from the *New Revised Standard Version of the Bible*, copyright 1989, Division of Christian Education of the National Council of the Churches of Christ of the United States of America. Published by Oxford University Press, Inc., New York. Used with permission. All rights reserved.

Catechesis of the Good Shepherd Publications is an imprint of Liturgy Training Publications (LTP). Further information about these publications is available from LTP or Catechesis of the Good Shepherd, 7655 Main Street, Scottsdale, AZ 85251; phone: 480-874-3759; email: cgsusa.org.

Text © 1998; revised 2017. Catechesis of the Good Shepherd. All rights reserved.

THE CATECHESIS OF THE GOOD SHEPHERD IN A PARISH SETTING: REVISED EDITION © 2018 Archdiocese of Chicago: Liturgy Training Publications, 3949 South Racine Avenue, Chicago, IL 60609; 800-933-1800; fax 800-933-7094; email: orders@ltp.org; website: www.LTP.org. All rights reserved.

This book was edited by Margaret M. Brennan. Michael A. Dodd was the production editor, and Luis Leal was the designer and production artist.

Photographs © John Zich

22 21 20 19 18   1 2 3 4 5

Printed in the United States of America

Library of Congress Control Number: 2018943950

ISBN 978-1-61671-423-9

CGSPAR2

CONTENTS

FOREWORD TO THE REVISED EDITION   v

INTRODUCTION TO THE ORIGINAL EDITION   vii

CHAPTER ONE
History   1

CHAPTER TWO
First Steps   9

CHAPTER THREE
Generosity   15

CHAPTER FOUR
The Atrium   25

CHAPTER FIVE
What to Offer in the Beginning   31

CHAPTER SIX
Handling the Changes   37

CHAPTER SEVEN
The Atrium within the Parish   49

APPENDIX 1
Excerpts from a Catechist's Letter to Tina Lillig   53

APPENDIX 2
The Characteristics of the Catechesis of the Good Shepherd: Thirty-Two Points of Reflection   57

NOTES   63

BIBLIOGRAPHY   67

ADDITIONAL CATECHESIS OF THE GOOD SHEPHERD PUBLICATIONS   69

FOREWORD TO THE REVISED EDITION

For twenty years now, this "little guide," as Tina Lillig called it, has shared practical wisdom and encouragement with many who are wondering just how to begin the Catechesis of the Good Shepherd (CGS) in a parish setting. More importantly, this book has helped many to experience the joy of being led by children into the Kingdom of Heaven. Much has happened in the CGS over the course of these twenty years. The catechesis has seen the flourishing of the mustard seed in its growth around the world. With this growth, we have also become even more essential as we approach the "meeting of the two mysteries," God and the child. A significant example of this deepening of our understanding is how we now present biblical texts to the children. The children are masters of essentiality and have taught us that we no longer need to narrate the text in our own words before announcing Scripture to them. Hence the need for revising this book.

Tina's friendship was transformative in my life, and I do miss her greatly. I remember well how often I would call Tina for advice on how to implement the Catechesis in our fast-growing parish in Gilbert, Arizona. She would always reassure me, and we would spend hours talking about the gift of the children in our atria. When I applied to join the Level III national course held in Prior Lake in 1996, I had written about my own parish. Tina asked if she could use part of that letter as an appendix to this book and if I had photos of the children in our atrium that could be shared. I was happy to oblige! It has been profoundly moving for me to revisit her words, and her friendship, in the revision of the book.

In Tina's introduction, she writes of how this book truly began in her experience of the Catechesis of the Good Shepherd in her life and in the life of her community. It gladdens my heart to think of her and how her wisdom and experiences have been a gift to so many for forty years, such a rich and full amount of time. May this "little guide" continue to support all those who seek to serve the spiritual life of children.

Mary Mirrione
National Director CGSUSA 2017

INTRODUCTION TO THE ORIGINAL EDITION

Though the writing of this little guide took place during the 1996–1997 academic year, in a sense it began twenty years ago. Back then I was a young wife and the mother of three small boys. Our family had a limited income—a starting teacher's salary. My husband, John, and I had both been blessed with education in Catholic institutions from elementary school through college. We wanted our sons to grow to love Christ and the Church, so we did the things that many Christian parents do: Eucharist on Sunday, prayers at the table and at bedside, an Advent wreath, children's books of Bible stories.

I first learned of what is now known as the Catechesis of the Good Shepherd when our children's Montessori school announced a training course for adults at a local college. At that time it was called "the Montessori approach to religious education," and the very simple and understated brochure really spoke to me. "Prepare the way of the Lord," it said, and it referred to the great spiritual capacity and hunger of young children, something I was observing in my own three.

I was disappointed when I saw that the course was to be held for three weeks during the summer of 1977, five days each week from 9 AM to 4 PM. At that time John drove a city bus during the summers to support our family until his teaching year began in the fall. His work schedule changed from day to day, with his next day's run written on a chalkboard in the bus barn at the end of each day. We had no money for child care, but we decided that we would pay the tuition for the course, even if I could only go two days a week, the two weekdays John usually had off.

The first day of the course came, and I was delighted that John's bus run was scheduled for the evening shift and I could go. That first morning I knew it had not been foolish to pay the tuition and come. I was hearing the Christian message as if for the first time. And for the rest of the week John was scheduled for all night shifts, something that had never happened for a summer driver.

The second week of the course, the same thing happened. I was able to go each day while John stayed with our children, and he worked at night.

By this time I was taking in the content of the course deeply, finding that the different strands of my life had prepared me in remarkable ways for what I was hearing: my experience with Montessori education through Project Head Start, my interest in theology, my study in Italy, my motherhood.

During the third week of the course, John was scheduled for all nights again. Neither John nor I will ever believe that this happened by chance. Though I didn't know it at the time, the Catechesis of the Good Shepherd was to be my life work and my ministry for at least the next twenty years. It would fill my life with amazement and wonder as I witnessed the responses of children and adults to the mystery of God.

The aim of this book is simply to help others experience the joy of being led to God by children. The Catechesis of the Good Shepherd shows us this path. In the United States it has already been implemented in Catholic and Episcopal churches, Montessori and parochial schools. At present there is growing interest from Catholic dioceses and large Catholic parishes, Episcopal dioceses and parishes, and a few churches of other Christian denominations. This little book has been prepared as a sort of guide for churches that ask, "How do we begin the Catechesis of the Good Shepherd in our parish?"

My work as a local church catechist and as director of catechesis for St. Giles Community in Oak Park, Illinois, has given me a parish perspective from which to view the religious life of children. Therefore I have tried to limit the scope of this book to what happens in a parish when it chooses the Catechesis of the Good Shepherd for its youngest members. There are wonderful books and writings by Sofia Cavalletti and others about the theological, theoretical, and methodological aspects of this catechesis. These relate, above all, the experiences with children in settings that use the catechesis. But this book offers more practical, step-by-step information to answer some of the questions a church might have. It may be of use to pastors, directors of religious education, parish staff members, parents, catechists, or anyone else interested in the great blessing that young children are to a parish community.

The first chapter addresses the question "What is the Catechesis of the Good Shepherd?" It offers a brief history and description of this approach. Chapters 2 and 3 consider how a parish might come to know and explore this catechesis and how parish members can support it. Chapters 4 and 5 discuss planning for and actually beginning the atrium, the place where the children meet, and some ways the program could develop. In chapter 6 we address the impact on the whole parish, and some of the changes that take place. Chapter 7 discusses how the catechesis is integrated in the overall life of a church and concludes with a note on ecumenism.

Many people have been part of this project. Thanks to Jeanette Lucinio, SP, a mentor, advisor, and professor who helped me in numerous ways. Her understanding of children and her love for parish ministry is greatly appreciated. Thanks also to the rest of the faculty of Catholic Theological Union for the fine example of scholarship and service that they give. Thanks to the many who have formed me in the Catechesis of the Good Shepherd: Sofia Cavalletti, Maria Christlieb, Gianna Gobbi, Lillian Lewis, and Rebekah Rojcewicz; the catechists from whom I continually learn; and above all the many children of St. Giles Community with whom I have listened and worked and prayed in the atrium. Special thanks to my sons, John, Mathias, and Thomas Lillig, who were my motivation to take my first catechesis course, and to my husband, John, who has accompanied me on this journey from the very first step.

It is my sincere hope that the body of literature on the spiritual life of children will continue to grow and that the experiences of children in parishes will contribute to it.

Tina Lillig

Tina Lillig (1945–2009) was our association's first national director. Tina helped to nurture the seed of this association so that it could put down deep roots and spread wide branches. Even now, her spirit is alive in our work and is particularly known through many of our publications and our annual journal. Whether she authored articles or books herself or worked behind the scenes in editing and shepherding the production of publications or the journal, Tina's gifts greatly contributed to the ongoing growth of CGS.

CHAPTER ONE

History

> The Catechesis of the Good Shepherd allows God to speak directly to the child.
>
> —a parent

Today's parish is getting used to surprises. Its leadership is becoming more collaborative and diverse—women and men, ordained and nonordained. A parish convent sometimes houses not only sisters but also a diocesan office or a few women who would otherwise be homeless. The mission of today's parish is broad, reaching beyond its geographical boundaries, and some of its parishioners might come from beyond those boundaries too. It is listening to its own spiritual hungers and gathering for times of prayer: centering prayer, Taizé prayer, Morning Prayer, and Evening Prayer. The Lectionary has a growing importance in the life of the local church. Young and old reflect on the Sunday readings.

Another gift that is beginning to appear in parishes is known as the Catechesis of the Good Shepherd. It is a way of religious formation for children that is quite different from the published programs. It does not use a catechetical series of books or take place in a classroom. In this approach there is a room prepared for the children in which every object is a help to knowing God. It is a place of simplicity and order, prayer and work, and community. Everything in this room, known as the *atrium*, is intended to be appropriate to the ages and sizes of the children who gather there. It is their religious needs that guide the catechesis. The atrium allows the children to come into contact with Scripture, the liturgy of the Church, and for the older ones, the whole of sacred history.

The Catechesis of the Good Shepherd is not new. It began in Rome in 1954 and has roots in the beginning of the twentieth century. To speak about its history is to speak about two women whose work is the foundation of the catechesis. The first is Sofia Cavalletti, a Catholic laywoman who lived and worked in Rome, a Hebrew scholar and a biblical scholar. She was also a writer, an educator, a lecturer, and a catechist who would gather weekly with a group of children in her *centro di catechesi*. Gianna Gobbi was her collaborator. She was a Montessori educator, a trainer of teachers, and a catechist of children. Her connection to Maria Montessori, the great Italian physician and educator, went back to 1951, when Gobbi assisted Montessori in a course in Rome.

Cavalletti has described their work, and the work of catechists in many countries, in the book *The Religious Potential of the Child*.[1] Although the focus of this book is the three-to-six-year-old, the Catechesis of the Good Shepherd nurtures the spiritual development of children through age twelve. There are several remarkable things about Cavalletti's book that draw the attention of religious educators, parish staffs, parents, and others who are interested in the spirituality of the child. One is her demonstration, through numerous examples, of the catechetical potential of children as young as three. Catechesis with the littlest children has become the real gift to the Church that is offered by the Catechesis of the Good Shepherd. Related to this is another of Cavalletti's insights. If we delay catechesis until the customary age of six, the child has moved into a new ethical stage in life when God is more likely to be perceived as a judge. Beginning to know God as a loving entity is easier for the younger child. And above all, the younger child is especially responsive to God's overture of love.

What also unfolds throughout the book with brilliance and clarity is the rightness of the themes offered to the young child. Cavalletti's choices of biblical passages and of moments in the liturgy come partly from her scholarship, but mostly from her wisdom and acute perception of the child. Her method is grounded in experience. In the beginning, she and Gobbi observed the reactions of the children. If the children were captivated by the subject and repeatedly drawn to the materials that made it concrete, Cavalletti and Gobbi concluded that the children's religious needs were being met. The interest, activity, and most of all the joy of the children guided and refined the curriculum. For more than four decades she had given children what seems most essential in the Bible and the liturgy.

> And so an ensemble of elements—few and essential—was slowly delineated, which the child showed that he knew, not in an academic way, but as if they were a part of his person, almost as if he had always known them. With the parables, for instance, some were set aside and reserved for an older age group,

and we concentrated on those parables that proved to be a constant object of the child's passionate interest.[2]

What happened in those early years to lead Cavalletti and Gobbi to this method? How did it happen that little by little an essential curriculum took shape, not at the desk of a religious educator or publisher, but in the encounter of children with Scripture and the liturgy?

Before Cavalletti began this work, her professional development had been greatly influenced by Dr. Eugenio Zolli.[3] Zolli had been the chief rabbi of Rome during World War II and was baptized a Christian in 1945. Cavalletti had taken Hebrew classes with Zolli and, after earning her doctorate, became his colleague. He is well known through his autobiography, *Before the Dawn*, which was published by Sheed and Ward in 1954, the same year Cavalletti began her work with children.

The Beginning

In March of 1954 Cavalletti began her catechesis work. Referring to this time, she said, "We started without knowing we started." A friend of Cavalletti had a child, a boy about seven years old. This woman asked Cavalletti if she would give the boy some lessons in religion. Cavalletti had never worked with children, but she agreed because of friendship and because it was a temporary arrangement. She began with this child and two other boys. She had no materials and no experience, only her Bible. She started by reading the first page of Genesis. Cavalletti says that she was deeply moved by their unexpected reaction of joy. They spent two hours just on that page.

This is entirely believable if one knows the rabbinical way of reading Scripture that formed Cavalletti, the way in which she forms others. Everyone is seated with open Bibles as colisteners to the word of God. Each phrase is pondered and wondered about with utter fidelity to the text.

A short time after this experience Cavalletti began her collaborative work with Gobbi, who brought a knowledge of Montessori education to the endeavor. Maria Montessori herself (1870–1954) had begun some religious work with children in Barcelona. There is a booklet narrating this work, *I bambini viventi nella chiesa* (1922), which preceded *The Child in the Church*, first published in 1929 and revised in 1965.[4] This volume describes Montessori's seminal work and its first offshoots in Europe and North America.

Gobbi was probably well acquainted with Montessori's religious work, especially with the use of materials designed for children. One day, when she and Cavalletti were scheduled to meet with the children, Gobbi brought in many packages. These were the first materials: a small model altar and articles used at Mass. Cavalletti says that the incredible joy of the children at their "awkward efforts" was the impetus for the pair to do something more organized the following year.

The first biblical material for the children was a Bible Cavalletti found in which each book was printed as a separate book. It was in French, since nothing similar was available in Italian.[5]

Cavalletti also speaks about the first time she had a revelation of the capacity of children for prayer and concentration. It was at Easter in 1955, the year of the liturgical reform of the Easter Vigil. As she watched the liturgy of the light—the new fire, the lighting of the Paschal candle, the spreading of the light to the assembly—she thought, "This seems to be made on purpose for children." That week she did the liturgy of the light with ten children. As one child put the grains of incense into the candle with immense care, there was an incredible silence. It was not an empty silence, but a "full" silence.

Little by little the children led Cavalletti and Gobbi to choose a "program." The Good Shepherd material, one of two pillars of the work, was there from the earliest days. It was probably the second biblical material. This wooden material, consisting of a sheepfold, shepherd, and ten sheep, was used for decades by hundreds of children without needing any repair. This was a sign of the deep respect the children had for the material.

The other pillar of this work is the True Vine, the great Christological parable in John 15, which is presented to children over six. It started with that first group of ten children. At that time, there was very little material in the atrium, so Cavalletti was reading with a child a prayer from the Missal. The prayer said, "Don't let us go far from you ever." To make it more clear, Cavalletti mentioned the True Vine. She did not read from the Gospel, but only mentioned it. The child remembered it again and again, so a vine plant was added to the atrium.

The Montessori base of the Catechesis of the Good Shepherd is most noticeable in the atrium. Even the word *atrium* was chosen by Maria Montessori herself, in 1922, when she added a room for the child's religious life to a school in Barcelona. Much earlier the word had been used for the entry to ancient Christian basilicas, the space where catechumens were prepared for Baptism.

In the early 1900s, the work of Maria Montessori uncovered characteristics and capacities of children that were not commonly known. She consistently wrote about the young child's love of order, capacity for concentration, desire for work, and most surprisingly, love of silence. The recognition of these characteristics is what inspires the atrium. The furniture is child-sized to foster moving about freely, working comfortably, and using and moving objects.

The qualities most noticeable about the materials in the atrium are their simplicity and their order. Each material has its own place on the Scripture shelf or on the liturgical shelf. There are other centers in the room as well—a Baptism area, an altar table, a geography area, a prayer corner. Above all, the room has a certain solemnity. The young child is shown how to walk slowly and speak softly so that, even though everyone is busy and active, an atmosphere of silence permeates the atrium.

Many catechists have observed that the atrium becomes even more important to older children. Rooms prepared for children from six to nine and nine to twelve become almost a refuge, certainly a respite from the pace and pressure of the modern child's life. The approximately two-hour sessions offer to children of all ages time to listen, work, pray, sing, wonder, rest, and discuss important things. In the silence of the atrium, children sometimes make a first discovery that they have an inner life.

The Good Shepherd

The Catechesis of the Good Shepherd takes its name from one of the earliest and most central presentations offered to children, the parable of the Good Shepherd (John 10:3–5, 11–16). The catechist, seated beside a low table with the children gathered around her, briefly introduces the parable. A candle is then lit, and the passage from the Bible is read.

The points on which we linger, for it is these that most enchant the children, are above all the personal love and protective presence of the Good Shepherd: He calls each one of his sheep by name, he knows each intimately even if there are many sheep; he calls his sheep and gradually they become accustomed to the voice of their Good Shepherd, and they listen to him. In this way a precious relationship is established; a thread of love binds the sheep always more closely to their Shepherd. The Shepherd's voice is powerful and supremely patient; it never tires of calling and reaches out even to those sheep who are far away, beyond the sheepfold. Slowly they too turn to hear his voice, and they gather together into one great flock. The Shepherd knows the needs of his sheep, and he guides them to good pastures, walking ahead of them to show the way and to be the first to confront any danger should it arise. So the sheep are safe and peaceful with their Good Shepherd; they know there is someone to protect them even in danger.[6]

The announcement is followed by a communal meditation during which the catechist poses a few open-ended questions: "These sheep of the Good Shepherd are so fortunate. They are loved so much. I wonder who they are?" Some children suggest sheep they have seen. Others begin to name people. The catechist will leave to them the discovery that we are the sheep. Often the children respond with only silence.

At this point the material is introduced. "This is the sheepfold." (It is placed on the table.) "This is the Good Shepherd. These are the sheep." The catechist reads the parable again, moving the material with very simple movements: placing the sheep in the sheepfold, the shepherd calling them out, the shepherd going ahead of them, the sheep following. This opens the way for them to work with the material later in the atrium session.

It is with this text that the children are introduced into the mystery of the person of Christ. It is primarily the children's responses that account for the choice of this parable.[7] The children work repeatedly with this material, moving it in their own way as they appropriate its truth. Here they show us, more than with any other piece of work, what it means to really pray with a material.

The children also teach us the importance of the Christocentric way of catechesis: to come to God through Christ. This is our religious reality, having been born into the time of redemption. And so religious experiences, and even the reading of the Old Testament, are always in this light.

Cavalletti mentions that that for a long time she thought the most powerful part of the Good Shepherd image was the protective aspect of the shepherd. It was an obvious thing because little children have a particular need to be protected, to feel secure. But as she studied their artwork she saw another element, fuller and deeper, and at the root of the sense of protection. It is the element of relationship. The sense of security is rooted in the relationship and is indeed a fringe benefit of that relationship. Later the child will encounter the depth of this relationship in the paschal aspect of the parable: "The Good Shepherd lays down his life for the sheep" (John 10:11).

The Good Shepherd parable can be basic in the formation of a moral person. It helps the child enjoy a relationship with God, a relationship of deep peace, a real relationship of being in love.

An International Movement

Evidence of the suitability of the Catechesis of the Good Shepherd for children of diverse cultures is its spread to many countries. Atriuwms exist in Argentina, Australia, Austria, Belgium, Bolivia, Brazil, Canada, Chile, China, Colombia, Costa Rica, Croatia, Cuba, the Czech Republic, Denmark, Ecuador, England, France, Germany, Guatemala, Haiti, Honduras, India, Ireland, Italy, Jamaica, Japan, Kenya, Lithuania, Malaysia, Mexico, New Zealand, Nicaragua, Norway, Pakistan, Panama, Papua New Guinea, Peru, Poland, Puerto Rico, Romania, Serbia/Bosnia, Singapore, Slovenia, South Africa, South Sudan, Spain, Sweden, Switzerland, Tanzania, Thailand, Trinidad, Uganda, the United States, Uruguay, Uzbekistan, and Venezuela. Cavalletti traveled to St. Paul, Minnesota, to give the first United States training course for adults in 1975. At that time, interest was primarily from Montessori teachers. She returned to the United States in 1978, 1982, and 1983. By the time she came again in 1984, interest had shifted significantly: now parish catechists and catechetical leaders were course participants. When Cavalletti returned in 1985, three Episcopalians were part of the group. Because of their leadership and enthusiasm, Episcopal parishes throughout the country now make up about 15 percent of Catechesis of the Good Shepherd atria. In 2016, 123 training courses serving Roman Catholic, Episcopal, and other church communities were offered in the United States.

Though guided by the same principles, atriums around the world are noticeably different. They reflect the conditions and characteristics of the place and of the culture, as well as the economic capacities of the parishes that organize them. But all carry the vision of the child's dignity and the child's desire to come closer to God.

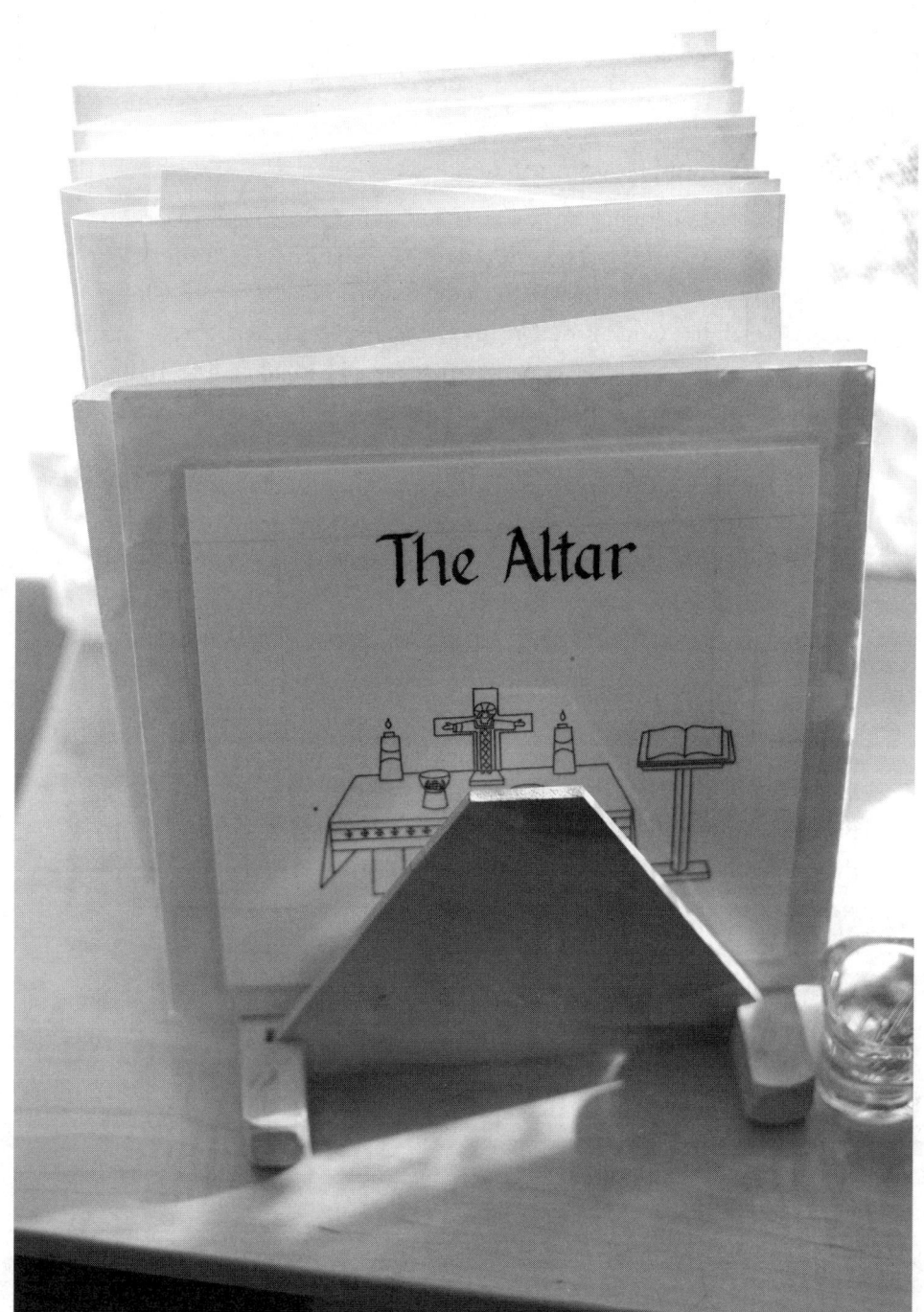

CHAPTER TWO

First Steps

> We are making the path as we walk in it.
>
> —a catechist

Who is it, in a parish, that first comes to know about the Catechesis of the Good Shepherd? It could be the parent of a young child. If an atrium exists in a neighboring parish, word begins to spread as parents talk to other parents. When a child longs for the next atrium session, displays a newfound love of silence, or searches the house for "holy things" to make a prayer corner, this is good news that must be shared. Sometimes it is a catechist who first is told about the atrium. Others know she is always interested in ideas about Christian education. It could be a teacher in the parish school or the director of religious education who is first handed one of the books that describes the catechesis. Or one of them may attend a workshop on a diocesan catechetical day.

Conversation about the Catechesis of the Good Shepherd has also been taking place at local meetings, national conferences, and Christian initiation weekends. Now and then it is the pastor or assistant pastor who takes a chance on a workshop session about preaching to the needs of children. Or he may hear of the catechesis from a priest at another parish.

Though the Catechesis of the Good Shepherd is not well known and carries with it the challenges inherent in that condition, somehow it is making itself known in all these ways.[8] Children are not part of these networks, and what they experience in the atrium cannot easily be put into words, but adults with even a slight acquaintance with this work are often quite affected. One unique aspect of the Catechesis of the Good Shepherd is that adults are drawn to and nourished by many of the presentations that are given to the children, just as the children are.

Exploring

Whoever discovers the program and is struck by it, parishioner or staff member, should probably make an appointment to tell the pastor about this approach to the religious formation of children. The outcome of this meeting would be to address a question of the heart: Can our parish explore this together? If the person initiating the conversation has already been to a training course, there is even more to discuss: the course and its effects, personal discoveries, all the imaginings of an atrium for children in the parish, and perhaps the sense of being called by God to this ministry.

Many other conversations may spring from this first one, as the pastor suggests others who might help. There may be informal discussions or meetings with the director of religious education, some catechists, a liturgist, and perhaps the entire parish staff. There is a growing understanding that parish life flourishes when all parish ministers work together and share a vision.[9]

The needs of the parish will surely influence these first meetings. Does a preschool religious education program already exist? If so, is there an openness to change? The usual way of beginning the Catechesis of the Good Shepherd is gradually, starting with children ages three to six. Though there are full curricula using this approach for children ages six to nine and nine to twelve, each level builds on the preceding one and results in a remarkable synthesis.[10]

A key element in the implementation of the catechesis is the involvement of the parents of the children to be served. Their parental love and their commitment to the Christian formation of their children open them to the possibility of conversion, both of themselves and of the whole Body of Christ.[11] Therefore, early in the process of exploring the catechesis, it is important to invite their partnership.

The most popular way to do this is to organize a book discussion group to read *The Religious Potential of the Child*. This can take place over a number of weeks and allow a group of adults to study, question, dream, and learn together. It seems good to cast a wide net in forming this group and to extend personal invitations to parents of recently baptized infants and toddlers. Grandparents, godparents, and any other interested parishioners may also be included as the parish comes to a deeper understanding of the spirituality of our children.

An alternative to Cavalletti's book is *The Good Shepherd and the Child: A Joyful Journey*.[12] This has been called a "parent-friendly" book. It is as profound as the other book, but simpler in its language and clearly organized within each chapter.

A book discussion group has many benefits. Whether or not the atrium becomes a reality, it is always fruitful when adults become more attuned to the religious needs and capacities of children. A small community may form as parents and other adults discuss things of the heart, and from that group might arise the desire for an atrium. Members of this core group may eventually embrace the work involved: preparing a room, making materials, fundraising to purchase shelves or to send a catechist for training.

There are additional ways for a parish to become more acquainted with the Catechesis of the Good Shepherd. Its national office offers a simple packet of basic information and an introductory booklet along with the many resources that can be found on the national website: www.cgsusa.org.[13] Visiting an existing atrium and talking to its catechists may be possible if there is one in the vicinity. Sometimes a catechist who has established an atrium is willing to come and speak about her experience, answer questions, and perhaps do one of the biblical or liturgical presentations. There are also introductory workshops springing up around the country.

After the initial exploration of the approach, some decisions need to be made. Can our parish send at least two catechists for training? Is there a room that can remain set up for the children throughout the year?

Formation

A radical departure from the usual formation of a volunteer catechist is the extensiveness of the formation in this catechesis.[14] Training is given on three levels; each level consists of at least ninety to one hundred hours. Level I explores the general principles of the Catechesis of the Good Shepherd, the history of the method and the religious capacity of the child, and develops themes most suitable for children ages three to six.

Level II concentrates on children ages six to nine. In order to take Level II, a catechist should have completed the training for Level I because the catechetical program for older children builds on what children have experienced in Level I. In Level I, only the essentials are shown to the child, in keeping with their developmental stage. Level II expands and elaborates on some of the same themes and adds some new themes.

Level III goes further, developing themes suitable for children ages nine to twelve.

The formation courses for catechists consist of several kinds of experiences:
- Learning theological, pedagogical, and psychological background information—usually in lecture format.
- Making actual presentations with suitable materials—to learn how to make presentations to the children.

- Practicing the presentations in the atrium.
- Making "album pages" for what might be described as a catechist's handbook.
- Learning how to make the materials necessary for the atrium.
- Reading background material.

Several different formats for courses have emerged in response to the many requests for formation. In Rome there are courses that last up to three years. The year-long parts of these courses consist of three-to-four-hour lectures each week, observation and practice in an atrium with children, personal consultation, work on album pages, and work with materials in the atrium.

In the United States, different methods are in use. Because of the phenomenal growth of the catechesis, it has been a challenge to bring formation to all who ask for it. The following are some of the formats:

- Concentrated summer courses. The ninety or more hours are divided into two summer sessions, each two weeks long, in two successive years.
- Five long weekends scheduled throughout one year. Local catechists may add extra days to this schedule if needed.
- One day per month, or one evening plus one day per month over the space of one year or eighteen months, on a more-or-less flexible schedule.
- In addition to the scheduled course work, participants usually do some or all of the following: observation and work in an atrium, observation in a Montessori school, work on the album, background reading, and making materials for their atrium.

Participants are often deeply affected by the training. One catechist wrote, "No one has ever laid out the faith for me like this." Another said, "Everything I ever hoped was true is true!" A lifelong Catholic commented, "Finally, I really know who I am praying to."

There are several important ways to support catechists who return from training ready to begin this ministry in the parish. The first is to appreciate that something new and good is happening in their lives that will grow even greater as they work with the children. They may find that they are open to God's presence in a fuller way. They may need conversation and prayer with others in ministry from time to time. This can truly be a blessing for a parish.

In many cases it is important that the parish subsidize the catechist's training, partially or fully.[15]

It is prudent for both catechist and parish to have at least two catechists take training. Unexpected changes do occur in people's lives, and it would be a sad thing to delay or abandon the establishment of the parish's atrium because their one catechist was unable to continue. The number of catechists to be trained will depend on the size of the parish and the possibility that after some experience those trained will be willing to guide future parish catechists.

Space

The decision about the room to be dedicated to the catechesis can be more difficult than it would seem at first. A large parish is served by many ministries, all of which have regular meetings. It may also serve as host to numerous support groups and other organizations for parishioners and guests of all ages. Indeed, the annual parish calendar meeting, when space is reserved for all these meetings and events, can be a challenge.

The thought of a dedicated space, reserved for only one purpose, could meet with some resistance. The key to answering this resistance would be more information about the atrium and the religious needs of the child to be honored in it. A less-than-perfect space that no one uses can be made into a beautiful atrium by the loving work of a group of parents, children, and catechists. Enthusiastic catechists have even begun in shared space, setting up the atrium and taking it down again for each meeting (In one church in Mexico, a catechist used the area in front of the altar on weekday afternoons!). But as the catechesis grows and parishioners make the materials for the fifty presentations that are given to the children ages three to six, this would become a real hardship.

The time of decision-making is also the time to begin communicating with the whole parish about the Catechesis of the Good Shepherd. Brief announcements in the Sunday bulletin inviting questions and providing answers, or distributing reprints of articles from *Assembly*, *Sojourners*, *Liturgy*, *Pastoral Liturgy*®, or *Our Sunday Visitor*[16] could inspire a parish to move over slightly and provide a space for God and the child to meet.

CHAPTER THREE

Generosity

> I am of the firm belief that the main requirement to have an atrium is to have a community of baptized Christians. From that you get enough gifts and blessings to make an atrium.
>
> — a catechist

Children call forth from adults a generous spirit. In a parish family, the opportunity for children to meet God in a personal way often brings forth a response that is more than we could ask or imagine. When the Catechesis of the Good Shepherd begins in a parish and then takes root, there are always costs—both money and time. Paradoxically, it is not like a program that can be simply bought and installed. Because of all its dimensions, it asks a little morsel of support from each member of a parish community.

Formation Costs

When a parish decides to start an atrium, the obvious questions are: What will it cost? and Who will do it? These two questions are related because, unlike other programs, one of the biggest expenses is the formation for the catechist. The tuition for the Level I formation course is roughly equivalent to the tuition for a course in a Catholic university, Christian seminary, or graduate school of ministry. It involves at least ninety hours rather than the thirty or thirty-six hours of class time for a university course. There are books, manuals, supplies, and equipment needed for the course, as well as other things that are useful but not necessary: for example, a camera for taking pictures of the materials, which will be helpful when materials are made for the parish.

In addition to tuition and books, the costs for the intensive summer courses (two weeks, two summers) may involve room and board at a college campus or retreat center, and air fare. There are also the costs of being away from one's employment or of child care.

But there are ways to ease some of these expenses. A few of the courses offer scholarships, especially for catechists from low-income parishes or those who intend to serve children in a needy area. Partial scholarships may also be available for participants who assist in the operation of the course by photocopying handouts, taping lectures, and the like. The national office also offers partial scholarships and grants for formation. With the surprising growth of the catechesis, there may be local courses, which would eliminate high transportation expenses. Courses offered on weekends may avert the need to take time from work or to find child care. One Catholic diocese in the Midwest awarded a generous grant to a year-long formation course, which resulted in lower tuition for all the participants.

Another substantial way that parish members can help is to provide meals and to care for the children of a parent who goes to training. This has touched the hearts of many catechists.

It is radical indeed for a parish to provide for the ministerial formation of a volunteer. And it is even more radical when the volunteer is preparing to work with three-year-olds! But this is one of many ways that the Catechesis of the Good Shepherd has been changing church communities, putting "a little child in their midst" (Mark 9:36).

Atrium Costs

If an atrium for the youngest children is to have a place in the life of a parish, it is usually wise for it to be part of the larger religious education program. Under this protective umbrella, the atrium will not be viewed as something extraneous or separate, but rather as part of the parish's total catechetical ministry. An arrangement like this acknowledges that all the baptized are a gift to the Church, and as soon as children can respond to God, we must give them the opportunity. Even the smallest ones have catechetical and pastoral rights.

Some of the needs of the Catechesis of the Good Shepherd can be met within the parish's education ministry. This ministry's budget often provides for the leadership of a director or coordinator, registration costs, recordkeeping, retreats and gatherings for catechists, and such necessary services as copying and mailing.

Once a room is chosen for the atrium, emptied and cleaned up, there are some things that must be made, purchased, or found: furnishings, carpeting, supplies, and the catechesis materials.

Furnishings can be a big expense, or they may be found within the parish. If the parish has ever had a preschool program, there may be small chairs and tables stored somewhere, as well as low shelves. If a parish-wide search is fruitless, furniture can sometimes be purchased very inexpensively. A catechist from a Chicago-area parish went to a sale at a neighboring parish and found small desks and chairs—for $2.50 each. She bought six desks and six chairs for $30, and two more chairs at $1 each. This was really all that was needed for a beginning atrium with twelve or fifteen children per group. Because the children choose their work and then work individually, not all the children are working at tables or desks at the same time. Some sit on the floor with their materials on a small rug in front of them. (Rugs can be found for a few dollars.) At the same time, another child may be setting the altar or preparing the prayer corner.

One parish in Mexico began by asking each family to send a small chair with their child. Most of the chairs were handmade. Tables were improvised and the atrium opened. Sometimes it may take a few years, but eventually suitable and inviting furniture will be found.

Shelves are always easy to locate in a parish. If parishioners are made aware that low wood shelves are needed, 10" to 14" deep, there will be many donations. Small wooden tables are also welcome—coffee tables or tables for lamps or plants. The challenge is to find things that are low, sturdy, and not in need of too much repair. Garage sales or rummage sales are good sources for good prices. A catechist who has been to training and is familiar with the atrium at the training course would be the best guide to what is appropriate.

If it is possible to purchase new furniture, a local Montessori school can suggest sources of good-quality, long-lasting items. But it is best to go slowly and learn what is needed by being with the children.

Silence is one of the characteristics of the atrium, and carpeting is a great help for this. Noisy areas can be quieted by a sound-absorbent rug. But carpeting can be a large expense for a room of four hundred to eight hundred square feet. Many times the catechesis begins with the carpeting as a goal yet to be realized. If the atrium is in a basement room, it may be necessary to install carpeting immediately for warmth and comfort. This is another need to bring to the awareness of parishioners. One parish received an excellent room-size rug from a member whose office was being recarpeted to match a new color scheme. The donation of a vacuum is also a blessing if there is not one available at the church.

Supplies for the atrium will be an ongoing expense. Drawing paper, colored pencils, glue, candles, and polish are among the supplies that will be needed. Other needs might include paint, rollers, and brushes for walls and shelves; dishwashing liquid, spray cleaner, and rags for keeping things clean. These things are often purchased, but they might be donated if parish members are given a specific list.

There are about fifty catechetical presentations given to the children ages three to six. Each presentation involves materials that are later used by the children in their personal activity. This offers them an aid to absorbing the theme that was presented. The materials are attractive but very simple. When catechists attend a formation course, one of the manuals they purchase contains measurements and directions for the handmade materials. A few of the materials can be purchased: a Good Shepherd statue for the prayer corner; glass, brass, and pottery things; and two or three wood items—the things that are more difficult to make (the city of Jerusalem model, a liturgical calendar with fifty-two wood prisms). These may seem like a great expense, but materials are best added to the atrium slowly, over the course of many years. Too many all at once would distract and overwhelm the children.

Gianna Gobbi has written that to the modern mind it seems to be quite odd and perhaps even a waste of time for catechists, parents, and other parishioners to make materials. But when materials are made with our own hands, we enter into the rhythm of human beings, not machines. This prepares us for the rhythm of children as they work with the materials. It also gives to all who prepare them a way to absorb deeply the Christian message that the material holds. The catechist or parent will find that through their preparation of the material, they are able to convey the Christian proclamation to the children in a more compelling way. Material making also offers a time of peace for those who do it.[17]

Even preparing the materials ourselves does cost some money. We need such things as wood, sculpting compound, fabric and thread, poster board,

and pens. Sometimes parishioners provide these things without expecting reimbursement. At the end of this chapter there are some examples of ways to invite parishioners to help.

An important thing to remember as we embrace the gift of material making is that the Catechesis of the Good Shepherd can be realized in whatever social and cultural environment it finds itself.[18]

A Mexican catechist wrote:

> Today, [in] 1983, Chihuahua has atria in two Montessori schools and in four parishes. Visiting them this summer we experienced in these rooms an atmosphere of prayer. They are filled with the presence of God and of the children. The material is beautiful, refined and very, very simple. You can see love in every object of the atrium; they have put together a great fidelity to the spirit and the material of Rome, and a creativity in using the things of the environment. We saw candlesticks made out of the tops of water bottles with a nail in the center.[19]

The reality of the atrium itself may also happen gradually. There is a flourishing catechesis in Minnesota that now has three large permanent atriums in a beautiful parish center. The catechists welcome children from age three up to age twelve. But this program had very small beginnings. In 1984 the catechist wrote:

Preschoolers meet at the church on Sunday morning. This atrium is in its second year. Materials are kept in a specially designed cabinet in a room used for other purposes during the week. An elementary class meets also on Sunday morning in a private home donated by one of the families in the program.[20]

Another decision to be made has to do with tuition for the atrium children. There are costs to the development and ongoing maintenance of a Catechesis of the Good Shepherd atrium, and tuition can help to cover these. But just as with all religious education tuition, no one should be excluded because of inability to pay.

The first years of the Catechesis of the Good Shepherd will become an often-recalled memory in the life of a parish. Finding a tiny vase at a rummage sale or emptying a parishioner's oil and vinegar down the drain to meet the need for cruets will become part of the stories of handing on the faith. It is important that the catechists not feel pressure to provide or prove the catechesis all at once. The children will respond with joy to the loving efforts of their parish family.[21] Even this simple list could be enough for the first year:

- the Good Shepherd material
- the small altar and articles of the altar
- a prayer corner (Good Shepherd statue, cloth, flower in vase, and candle on a small table)
- drawing paper and colored pencils
- mustard seeds
- a Nativity set from someone's home for the Annunciation presentation and the Birth of Jesus presentation
- a Paschal candle and small candles for the children, with one tiny white garment for the Baptism presentation
- a glass plate, a wine glass, and a cloth for the presentation on the epiclesis and offering/doxology gestures in the Mass
- a Bible

Other things can be easily added from week to week such as prayer cards and supplies for practical life activities like flower arranging and brass polishing. But with these few materials, the door of the atrium can be opened, and the Catechesis of the Good Shepherd can begin.

Example 1

Form for parents to fill out at registration

Name_____

Phone_____

Email_____

The catechesis materials, activities, and environments are the result of the outpouring of many gifts. *Please check the gifts you are able to offer:*

- ❏ I am a catechist.
- ❏ I am a substitute or sacramental catechist.
- ❏ I would like more information about becoming a catechist.
- ❏ Making small materials from wood
- ❏ Making small figures from clay
- ❏ Painting small materials
- ❏ Calligraphy
- ❏ Sewing
- ❏ Embroidery
- ❏ Cutting collage pieces out of construction paper
- ❏ Shopping for supplies
- ❏ Hosting meetings
- ❏ Musical ability:_____instrument_____song leading
- ❏ Cleaning atrium environment
- ❏ Computer work
- ❏ Phone calls
- ❏ Other: Please tell us if there are other ways you would like to help the catechesis program.

Example 2

Bulletin announcement

Catechesis Needs

Even though the catechesis year has just ended, we are already planning for next year. At an end-of-year meeting, we were offered a third atrium. Next year we'll have separate atriums for ages 3 to 6, ages 6 to 9 and ages 9 to 12. With this news, we also have some needs:

- a small low table for a prayer table
- shelving: two units of three or four shelves at least 10" deep
- school desks or small tables at which one or two children could work
- wine glasses for the celebration of the Last Supper: We could use 30 small, heavy glasses.
- someone who can sew two rugs together or could let us know where we could bring them to be sewn: Each rug measures 6'10" × 3'4".
- someone to make 12 pencil trays —wood block with three grooves for three pencils
- cloths—white, purple, green, red (bright liturgical shades): The cloths need to be about the size of a cloth napkin, place mat, or 30-inch runner. Any help with these needs would be greatly appreciated.

Example 3

Bulletin announcement

To the parents of the 3-to-6-year-old children:
During April and May the children are very interested in flower arranging in the atrium. If you have any spring flowers in your garden, we would all be very appreciative if you could send a few stems with your child. Thanks!

Example 4

Bulletin announcement

Atrium cleanup will begin May 18 for the 6-to-9 and 9-to-12 atriums and June 1 for the 3-to-6 atrium. This involves washing shelves and tables and cleaning each piece of the materials. We then cover everything for the summer. This cleanup is important because many hands use the materials throughout the year. If you can give an hour or two, please call _____ to find out the days or evenings we'll be working.

Thanks!

CHAPTER FOUR

The Atrium

> I could live here.
> —a child

It may seem that these chapters are devoting an excessive amount of text to the subject of a prepared room for the children. Deep down, we know that the preeminent environment for Christian formation is people—family, the Christian community, godparents, and catechists. But anyone who has ever been a religious education teacher, an initiation catechist, a high school youth minister, or a teacher of religion in a parish school knows how it feels to make do with a less-than-suitable physical environment. Many people have concluded that catechesis is more effective when we pay attention to its environment.[22]

In early Christianity, churches were constructed with a room-size porch or entryway (an atrium) for the instruction and nurturing of those to be initiated. Christian symbols decorated its walls, so eye and ear were awakened to the sensory learning that is the method of the Church.[23]

In May of 1927, Maria Montessori elaborated on the concept of the atrium in a conversation with her biographer E. M. Standing, a teacher and writer:

> **Question:** Might not this idea of having a separate room for the teaching of religion be looked upon as rather unnecessary and newfangled?
>
> **Dr. Montessori:** People might think it was a new idea, but, as a matter of fact, it is a very old idea—almost as old as the church itself. In the early church there was, indeed, a special room called the atrium, generally adjoining the church, which was used for the training and instruction of catechumens. It was, as you might say, a sort of anteroom to the church, both in a literal and a metaphorical sense. Here, as in so many cases, we can with great profit take a "leaf out of the book" of the early church. This room then, which one might call the atrium, would be set apart for the preparation of little children for their full participation in the life of the church. It would not simply be a question of teaching them their catechism, but something much broader and deeper. This room would be a place

where the religious sentiment would be born and nurtured, where the children would be free in the expression of their religious instincts.[24]

Through the various activities of the atrium, children are helped to know "the great realities of life as a Christian."[25] They listen to stories of events in Jesus' life; they meditate on his parables while moving figures of sheep or holding a mustard seed; they paste cut-out shapes of Galilee, Samaria, Judea, and Perea to form maps; they cut and arrange flowers for the prayer corner; they clean candles; they set the altar; they pour macaroni, then lentils, and finally water and wine; they mix yeast and water with flour and watch it rise; they hold up the plate and cup in the Eucharistic gesture of offering; they write out Jesus' maxims; and they make drawings, such as the one a five-year-old made of the baby in a manger on an altar table. They do these things and many more, as well as pray, sing, and wonder. The atrium is full of life and well worth the effort of inaugurating it.

What kind of room is needed? A room the size of a classroom in a school will probably be just right. A room of 400 square feet is comfortable for twelve to fifteen children and two adults. A room of 600 or 800 square feet is even better. It allows for more children. It gives adequate space for the various centers for Eucharist, Baptism, prayer corner, Scripture, practical life, geography, and so on. A large room can eventually hold all the materials for the three-year curriculum. Children will be able to move about freely and unroll working rugs with ease. But smaller spaces are also workable. A room in the church basement allows easy access to the church. A room with windows lets in the beauty of natural light. It is always a blessing if the atrium is in a quiet area, but it should not be so remote that parishioners cannot observe and enjoy its life.

In a parish with many young families, another question about the atrium comes up: Should there be one or more than one? Several different groups of children can be served in one atrium, but scheduling sessions without undue inconvenience to catechists and families will be an annual chore. One very large suburban parish in the Midwest had eighty preschoolers who wanted to register for the Good Shepherd program. The parish decided on four groups of twenty, two groups on Saturday and two on Sunday. A smaller church with forty children established four groups of ten. One session was on Saturday mornings and three were on weekday afternoons. A very large Episcopal parish in the South furnished and supplied six separate atriums that all met at the same time.

Often, when a church program for children ages three to six is implemented, the assumption is that the sessions will be held during a well-attended Sunday Eucharist. The Catechesis of the Good Shepherd sometimes begins in this way. But after a year or two, parents find that their children really want to be at Mass. Many of the liturgical presentations in the atrium (the gestures of epiclesis, offering/doxology, and peace; the preparation of the cruets and chalice, the washing of the priest's hands, the Last Supper, the liturgical colors) give the child an interest in and even a longing for the Mass. Hunger for Eucharist may begin to grow very early. Usually, when young children who have developed an interest in the Mass do attend, they do not pay attention for the whole time. But because of the atrium work, they now have some linking points to watch for and enjoy. Atrium sessions scheduled at a time other than during Mass also can have a more ideal duration: ninety minutes—or better, two hours.

Care of the Atrium

If a parish has the gift of many children, several groups of children may use the same atrium. While the size of the room and the style of its furnishings can vary greatly, the way the atrium is cared for matters most. It matters that the materials are simple and clean, pencils are sharpened, vases are clean and ready for new flowers, paper in the various sizes needed is in place, and tables are clean and not sticky. The peaceful, quiet work of the children somehow depends on these things.

The importance of the care of the atrium and materials becomes apparent as parents and catechists observe what this means to the children. "Isn't it beautiful?" said one four-year-old as she stood with her mother at the threshold of the atrium. Another child, age three, confided to his mother, "I could live here."

Just like the home of any normal family or the church building belonging to the parish family, no atrium will ever be perfectly clean and organized. But a well-cared-for environment is a real help for the children. They can work more independently without the need for frequent assistance from the adults to find things that are missing. They begin to "own" the atrium. They return materials that a younger child put in the wrong place. They set aside a broken pencil and get more paper when they use the last piece.

For the catechists, too, it is better when everyone works together to keep the atrium beautiful. They grow to appreciate how each material should be made, revealed, used, returned, and maintained.

What are some things that can be done to prepare the atrium, especially if more than one group of children uses it? Every catechist develops a little routine to follow before the children arrive. The preparation routine for a complete atrium for ages three to six might look like this:

- Prepare the materials for the presentation.
- Wet the sponges for flower arranging, polishing.
- Put out fresh flowers and fill the water pitcher.
- Set out wine and water.
- Make sure there is enough flour, yeast, and warm water.
- Check paper and colored pencils.
- Fill a small container with warm water to hold used glue brushes.
- Set out the attendance sheet.
- Pray.

Each catechist's routine will be particular to the atrium and to the ages of the children.

The atrium also needs to be cleaned and maintained regularly during the year. How often this is done depends on the need and on how many children use the room. This regular maintenance usually involves

- cutting new paper;
- sharpening pencils;
- checking the materials;
- washing tables;
- dusting shelves;
- laundering cloths;
- sweeping or vacuuming the floor.

At the end of the year, all linens are laundered, and each material is cleaned and covered for the summer. Then in the fall, the catechists can simply uncover the materials, polish the brass things, and get ready to greet the children.

Many catechists and parents enjoy cleaning the atrium. Some like to work in silence, and others talk together or listen to music while they work. It can also be a time of prayer:

O God, may the small hands that hold these pencils draw what you have written in their hearts.

Thank you, God, for Sarah, who loves to fill this vase with flowers. May she always be filled with your praise.

May the child who will pour from these cruets help to lead us all into your mystery.

Example 5

Checklist posted in the atrium

Catechists,

Before leaving the atrium, please:
- Check floors for paper.
- Wipe off tables.
- Wash used bowls, cruets, polish holders, glue brushes, etc.
- Put away matches.
- Put new liner in waste basket and take trash to dumpster.
- Close windows.
- Check washrooms.
- Turn lights out.

Thank you!

CHAPTER FIVE

What to Offer in the Beginning

> The Catechesis of the Good Shepherd is a slow, deep process, full of God's peace.
> —a director of children's ministries in an Episcopal church

A parish sister recently asked: "Do you start with just three-year-olds? Could you start with six- and seven-year-olds?" She also wanted to know if the catechesis could "function in a school with five-and six-year-olds."

Even a brief acquaintance with the Catechesis of the Good Shepherd leads to the conclusion that children of all ages could benefit from this approach. Teens and adults as well have been deeply touched when they see any of the fifty presentations that are intended for children ages three to six. The utterly simple expression of these essential Christian themes from Scripture and the liturgy has an impact that is not easily forgotten.

Sometimes children older than six experience these first presentations. A new atrium with a small number of children may stretch the age limits a bit. Or a parish might establish a group for older children that will begin by using the same curriculum but adapted for the older child (for instance, with more written work, copying the actual Scripture, and so on). But it quickly becomes apparent that older children have different needs. Their image of Jesus as the Good Shepherd is now not only that of a protector and caregiver, but also of a hero who lays down his life for the sheep. They want to synthesize what they already know from the liturgy and the Bible. They hunger for a cosmic vision of reality and to know "Who am I in this world?" So they need to hear the announcement of one vast sacred history. They also want the teachings of Jesus that tell us how to love God and love other people. As these needs present themselves, a catechist who has taken only a Level I formation course will certainly be motivated to continue with the next level of training.

It is more difficult when a parish wants to begin the atrium with only children of age six and older. Sometimes this happens because the age of six or seven is commonly defined as the "catechetical age." Throughout the world, authors have published outlines of the developmental stages of faith that place younger children in an "immature preliminary stage."[26] The Good Shepherd approach, rooted in the Montessori discovery that the child has capacities no one had thought possible, allows for another vision. The young child has a great hunger for God and is especially responsive to the overture of God's love. Within the littlest child is the capacity to enjoy a relationship with God deeply. Our task is to discover and protect these treasures in the child that lead to fullness of life (John 10:10). What is available in the atrium is simply time and space for God. As the child grows and falls in love with the Good Shepherd, the child will want to know everything about this beloved person: where he grew up and lived, who his friends were, what he did and said. Little by little the child is drawn to share the life of Christ.

Another difficulty with establishing the Catechesis of the Good Shepherd only for older children, using the Level I presentations designed for ages three to six, is that very soon the catechists will want to try the work with the younger children it is intended for. Other churches will be welcoming the little ones, and the parish's three-year-olds will be drawn to the atrium. Once it is established, how can we turn them away? The older ones will want to continue once they have started, and the catechists might feel pressure to take the Level II training and make the new materials suitable for ages six to nine. It seems best to begin slowly, with the youngest children. When the Catechesis of the Good Shepherd comes to a parish, the great gift it brings is its focus on the young child and the covenant the young child is truly able to live.

A church can keep the atrium for only the children ages three to six for a long time. Many parishes do. In fact it is a big decision to open an atrium for the children ages six to nine and nine to twelve. Each level requires further training for the catechist, another room, more materials, and supplies. But the cost of the textbooks that are used in other catechetical approaches is eliminated, and for a large program that is substantial.

What usually compels a parish to extend the Good Shepherd curriculum for school-age children? Usually it is the children themselves, who have come to love their time in the atrium. As they grow older, they hunger to go deeper into the world of the Bible and the liturgy. They have grown to love the

parables of Jesus and are now ready for the moral parables. They have learned to explore parables in a different way than that offered by most textbook approaches. They want to hold the actual Bible and reflect on it in an open-ended way. Prayer, the history of this kingdom Jesus spoke about, and the origin of Eucharist and its cosmic dimension are themes they yearn for. But what really matters is the "I-Thou" relationship of the atrium that sometimes escapes other catechetical programs.

Another factor that drives the extending of the program is its approach to the sacraments. Many parishes find themselves seeking to follow a model for completing the initiation of children that is less school-based and more closely related to the catechumenate. They see that the atrium is grounded in the catechumenate down to its very name. Many of the components of first Eucharist in the Catechesis of the Good Shepherd seem natural to parishes that take Christian initiation seriously: the retreat for the children

immediately before the sacraments, the presentation of the gospel, the "handing over" and "return" of the Our Father, all the children—boys and girls—in the white garment, and so on.

The catechesis can expand to include older children quite smoothly if the parish does some careful planning and the pace is unhurried. The best time is probably when the atrium for ages three to six is well established and enthusiasm is high. Some parishes plan to begin the next level when the first three-year-olds are about to start first grade. Other approaches have also been tried. For example, a catechist for ages three to six could be sent to Level II training and could then work with the parish's annual first Eucharist program until an atrium for ages six to nine could be opened. The key is a "slow . . . process, full of God's peace."

If a parish implements the full catechesis for children ages three to twelve, a new need may come to the surface: someone to direct or coordinate it. The continuing gift of three atriums is a very big project, usually requiring a full-time director or coordinator. Often the current director of religious education can take on this role, as more and more DREs are taking the formation courses. In a very large parish where the Catechesis of the Good Shepherd is the sole religious formation program for all children until junior high, the employment of an assistant or administrative assistant also may be necessary.

Expanding the atrium from preschool to school-age children involves articulating the catechesis to an even larger group of parents. Part of the decision to develop atria for older children involves knowing what form of religious education parents want for their children. Some parishes begin the Catechesis of the Good Shepherd as a pilot program. One very wise DRE in a large Midwestern parish guarded against division by offering the atrium for ages six to nine as one of three options: a traditional book-based program, a home-based "family catechesis" model, and the Catechesis of the Good Shepherd. She found that most parents are accustomed to having options in today's educational systems and welcomed the choices.

It can take years to implement the catechesis for all the parish children from age three up to age twelve, with a group of trained catechists, sufficient space for the atriums, and all the necessary materials and furnishings. But the life of the atrium is so rich that it is hardly ever ended once it has begun.

CHAPTER SIX

Handling the Changes

> The Catechesis of the Good Shepherd will never make it in the Catholic Church. But if it did, it would be a revolution.
>
> —a catechist

Whenever a church begins the Catechesis of the Good Shepherd, there is change. Even if the catechesis does not replace another curriculum, but is merely added where there had been no preschool program, something is no longer the same. The birth of the new atrium is usually accompanied by great interest and excitement. But it can also be a bit unsettling because it is not familiar. The experience of change is seldom easy.

One thing that seems to happen in a parish with a new atrium is a new look at the child and the child's religious needs. When young parents participate in a four-to-six-week discussion of one of Cavalletti's books, conversions often happen. There can be a conversion to God as these adults recall the first flame of faith in their early lives, and also even a "conversion" to the child. Many begin to see children as "subjects" rather than objects to be filled with religious knowledge.[27] We can teach children the words and the prayers, but what children really come to know in a lasting way must first be in their hearts. We cannot control the way children perceive and interpret what we proclaim.[28] But we can give them a place to gather and to be quiet, and there nourish them with God's own way of revelation: Bible and liturgy.

One of the characteristics of the Catechesis of the Good Shepherd is the "de-schooling" of catechesis. This move away from the school model seems confusing at first, but the perspective of history makes it a little clearer. Religious education has always been intimately related to and influenced by the times in which it takes place. This statement is so simple, but its truth seems amazing. What is left out of religious education (for instance, in the *Didache*, a document on Christian teachings from about the year 70, no specific mention is made of the Body and Blood of Christ so that the emperor's spies would not report anything strange about the Christians) and what is restored (such as the word *catechesis*) depend on current dangers, movements, social science discoveries, reactions to previous times, and the needs of peoples and cultures. Some readers of these chapters have lived through different times: the time of the *Baltimore Catechism*'s "definitions," then the more experimental time soon after the Second Vatican Council. We inherited a school model or classroom model of religious education that was an offshoot of the Catholic school movement in the United States. This movement is important in our history because of the need to reinforce a strong Catholic identity. Therefore, in many places textbooks, workbooks, desks, schoolrooms, and teachers are the tools of catechesis.

The implementation of the Rite of Christian Initiation of Adults, which has restored some of the earliest wisdom of the Church, began in the 1970s and has gained enormous momentum since the late 1980s. It has brought us new words and new ways, many of which are the words and ways of early Christianity. Such concepts as process, formation, community, the involvement of many, conversion, initiation, liturgy, and relationship have found their way into these pages because of Christian initiation in our time and because they describe the approach of the Catechesis of the Good Shepherd.[29]

One change that comes with the atrium is a change in vocabulary. Instead of *teacher*, it is "catechist," "session" rather than *class*, "presentation" rather than *lesson* (except where *lesson* has a specific liturgical meaning, as in the Episcopal tradition). The children form a "group" rather than a *class*, and even the little ones "work" rather than *play*. One way to promote growing together into new words and new attitudes could be with regular letters to parents and parishioners, some examples of which are found at the end of this chapter.

The curriculum of the catechesis follows the liturgical year and the usual textbook is absent. It also differs from a Lectionary-based program because it is not the Sunday readings from the Lectionary that dictate the presentations. What drives the program is the religious needs of the child at various stages of development. These have been demonstrated by children themselves in more than forty years of research. Seasonal presentations are made in the appropriate season: infancy narratives from Matthew and Luke during Advent and Christmas Time, parables of mercy and forgiveness during Lent, Passion narratives close to Holy Week, Baptism during Easter Time.

Because the content of the Catechesis of the Good Shepherd does not come from a catechetical textbook series, it might be difficult for parishioners to understand the religious formation and learning about the faith that is embedded in this approach. To address this, a catechist returning from training can provide a list of the presentations in each three-year cycle. The whole Level I curriculum is outlined according to the liturgical year in *The Good Shepherd and the Child: A Joyful Journey*. The three-year curricula for Levels II and III have not yet been gathered into a book and published in English, but the catechist can provide them. Usually the catechist's "album" or handbook is kept in the atrium. There is an album page for each presentation, with doctrinal points, direct and indirect aims, materials descriptions, and important points to focus on during the presentation.[30] Most parishioners become familiar with the content of the catechesis by enjoying the atrium over time and looking at the materials for each theme on the shelves. Those who visit frequently notice quickly when a new material has been added.

Another radical change is that the Catechesis of the Good Shepherd requires serious training in an area of ministry that usually asks for little professional preparation. Parishes are used to sending catechists to an annual workshop and a formation program designed and mandated by their diocese that results in some form of certification. It is rare for a parish to budget a full course's tuition for a volunteer catechist. Even if the catechists pay for the training course from their own resources, the mere fact that this depth of formation is required brings about a shift in thinking. Ministry to the littlest members of the parish is seen in a new light.

It is helpful when the parish staff can openly discuss the issue of formation for ministry. A large parish usually has a few paid professionals and many volunteer ministers. The staff may need to talk over several topics. What are the real needs and priorities of the parish at this time? Who else in our parish is called to pursue a deeper ministry formation? How does this fit with the mission of this particular parish? The answers to these questions may have surprising results. In addition to the catechesis training, new budget items may appear and old ones may vanish. A music minister may take a course on starting a youth choir. A Christian initiation team may attend a training focused on the Rite of Christian Initiation of Adults together, or a justice ministry might be enlivened because a recently retired parishioner is now free to make a commitment to year-long training.

As the Catechesis of the Good Shepherd grows to include older children and perhaps the parish school children, a new hurdle is faced. The catechesis may now require adding a paid staff member even though the current structure might not have room for this. This challenge has been met with honesty and justice in many churches. Changes are made, year by year, as the parish begins to "own" the catechesis and recognize it as the gift it is.

Example 6

Sample letter to parents

December, 20XX

Dear Parents,
Once again, the precious season of Advent has come into our lives and also into the atrium. At our first session this month, our prayer corner was still prepared for Ordinary Time when the children entered the atrium—the Good Shepherd statue was on the green cloth with a small candle. Now we have the Advent wreath on a purple cloth. The change was made by the children—each one carrying candle or wreath or purple cloth—as they slowly walked in procession to the music of Pachelbel. It was beautiful!

We also presented one prophecy: "The people that walked in darkness have seen a great light" (Isaiah 9:1). We spoke about "light" coming in a special way at Christmas.

This week we presented the Annunciation to Mary. Our beautiful figures of Mary and the angel Gabriel are simple, unbreakable, and very inviting. I expect the children will work with this material quite often. In a quiet bedtime moment, you might want to begin to pray with your children: "Hail, Mary, full of grace." (One line is enough for the littlest ones. Older ones can add, "The Lord is with you.")

Everyone seems to be working well. At the last session we added the polishing work—very popular work in the atrium. You are invited to come with your child to our Christmas season children's liturgy on Tuesday, December

28, at 6:45 PM, at St. Giles church. These liturgies really complete the atrium. Celebration is the way we touch God.

"Come, Lord Jesus, come and be born in our hearts" (from an atrium song).

Love,

_____

Example 7

Sample letter to parents

January, 20XX

Dear Parents,

"I want to tell you how I use the star," a five-year-old child said to the catechist. She held the two-inch comet star and moved it toward the stable. With the other hand she moved the figures of the Magi. She moved the star again and the Magi followed, advancing six more inches toward the stable. This was the way she worked with the material after the presentation of the Adoration of the Magi. This work has great value. It provides the children with movement, time for retelling the story to themselves, time to ponder, time to deepen.

The children have been thinking since November about the sheep of the Good Shepherd. "They are so precious. I wonder who they are," the catechist said. Perhaps this month the children will move a little closer to the great discovery of who the sheep are. We present the parable of the found sheep (Luke 15:4–6), recalling first what we had already heard about the Good Shepherd. Then we read in Scripture what Jesus would do if one of the sheep was lost. This is a profoundly rich and moving parable for both children and adults.

The children are working well. In addition to their work with the biblical and liturgical materials, they are drawing, arranging flowers, polishing, making collages, and some are tracing. Next month we will add the folding exercises.

Important dates:

Parent night, Friday, January 27, 7:00–8:00 PM, atrium.
Eucharist for the children, Friday, March 17, 4:00–5:00 PM, atrium.

May the new year be filled with many blessings.

Love,

_____

Example 8

Page from a catechist's album (handbook)
    I. **Title:** The Parable of the Leaven
    II. **Category:** Parables of the Kingdom
    III. **Age:** 3 years and up
    IV. **Sources:** Matthew 13:33; *The Religious Potential of the Child,* by Sofia Cavalletti (LTP), chapter 8; *The Good Shepherd and the Child: A Joyful Journey,* by Cavalletti, Coulter, Gobbi, and Montanaro (LTP), chapter 7; Catechesis of the Good Shepherd Level I courses in St. Paul, MN (1985), Toronto (1986–1987), Glen Ellyn, IL (1988–1989)
    V. **Liturgical time:**
    Optional, usually after Christmas Time and before or during Lent
    VI. **Doctrinal point:**
    Like the parable of the mustard seed, this parable reveals the mysterious nature of the Kingdom of God. The Kingdom is where there is a passage from less to more, the mystery of the growth and transformation that occurs because of God's strength of life. It involves work and waiting. Though often hidden, this strength transforms everything.
    VII. **Direct aim:**
    To announce to the child the mystery of the Kingdom of God as a mystery of life—that is, a small thing that develops.

VIII. **Indirect aims:**
   1. To help the child discover that the parable reveals the secret of creation: There is an energy in the universe that surpasses every human capacity.
   2. To help the child marvel at the Kingdom of God and the great happiness of belonging to it.
   3. To help the child enter into the mystery of life and death.
   4. Education to wonder.
   5. Moral formation based on love and joy in front of the mystery of the Kingdom of God.

IX. **Description of material:**
   - Bible or Scripture booklet with the Gospel text of Matthew 13:33
   - tray
   - small bowl
   - container with flour (small amount of sugar in the flour)
   - container with yeast (active dry yeast or quick rise yeast)
   - thermos with hot water
   - 1 tablespoon measure
   - 1/4 teaspoon measure
   - a leveler (straight edge to level flour)
   - a stick to stir with
   - a cloth or bowl to cover dough
   - tracing packet

X. **Presentation:**
   Introduce the parable by recalling other parables of the Kingdom. Focus on the mustard seed (Mark 4:30–32). Show Bible or Scripture booklet, read the parable of the leaven solemnly. Following the reading of the text, invite the children to recall what Jesus has told us.
   Meditation:
   What could Jesus have meant?
   How could that tiny bit of yeast make dough get bigger?

Presentation of material:
Say, "We can do what the woman did."
Pour some water from the thermos into the pitcher.
Show yeast and invite children to smell it.
Show flour and measure 3 tablespoons.
Add 1/4 teaspoon yeast.
Stir.
Show children mixture and ask them if they can see the yeast.
Add a little water (about 2 tablespoons).
Stir, cover. Tell the children we won't look until it is time to go home.
After the dough has had time to rise, gather with the children to wonder over how it has been transformed. Reread the parable.
Song: "Jesus, Remember Me" or "Seek Ye First"

XI. **Work of the children:**
1. free drawing
2. preparation of dough with the yeast and water
3. tracing packets
4. sequence cards
5. reading or listening to the parables of the mustard seed or pearl
6. writing these short parables

Example 9

Page from a catechist's album (handbook)

I. **Title:** Baptism II — The Word, the Water, and the Oil
II. **Category:** Baptism
III. **Age:** 3 years and up
IV. **Sources:** Matthew 28:19; John 1:12–13; Romans 6:3–11; II Corinthians 5:17; Galatians 3:26; Ephesians 5:8–14; Titus 3:4–7; 1 Peter 3:18–22; Rite of Baptism; *The Religious Potential of the Child*, by Cavalletti, chapter 5; *The Good Shepherd and the Child: A Joyful Journey*, by Cavalletti, Coulter, Gobbi, and Montanaro, chapter 8; Level I courses in St. Paul, MN (1985), Toronto (1986–1987)

V. **Liturgical time:**
Easter Time, usually after the presentations of the Prophecy of Light (Isaiah 9:1), the Good Shepherd, the Liturgy of Light, and Baptism I

VI. **Doctrinal points:**
Baptism is the participation in the death and resurrection of Christ. In Baptism we become children of God. Baptism has a Trinitarian dimension. Light, the white garment, word, water, oil, and all they signify are gifts of God. The Church is the sheepfold into which we are born, welcomed, and loved at Baptism.

VII. **Direct aims:**
1. To help the children read the baptismal signs.
2. To help the children fall in love with the Risen Christ and reflect on their Baptism with joy.

VIII. **Indirect aims:**
1. To help the children participate more fully in the liturgy.
2. To offer a vision of the Parousia through the spread of the light.
3. Moral formation.

IX. **Description of material:**
- Paschal candle, candle holder
- individual candles, holders
- matches
- candle snuffer
- white garment
- Bible and stand or lectern
- baptismal font or bowl of water
- a shell for pouring water
- small white towel
- oil of catechumens (or olive oil)
- chrism (or olive oil with fragrance added)
- white cloth for table

X. **Presentation:**
Introduce the presentation by recalling Baptism I—
the Light and the White Garment:
1. Recall the important day in our lives, the day of Baptism.
2. When Jesus was born, a light came into the world. (Light Paschal candle.)

3. When Jesus died, the light was extinguished. (Extinguish.)
4. Jesus is risen. The light of the Risen Christ entered the world and can be shared with everyone.
   (Relight Paschal candle.)
5. We received the light at Baptism. (Children can light individual candles from Paschal candle. Individual candles can be put in holders.)
6. (Show white garment.) A white garment was put on us to show we received the light.

Show and explain the signs of word, water, and oil.
1. Bible: has in it the Word of God. Some words from the Bible were read on the day of Baptism.
2. Water: Priest poured water over your head. (Pour water over your fist three times silently and again three times with the words: "I baptize you in the name of the Father, and of the Son, and of the Holy Spirit.")
3. (Invite children one by one to pour water over their own fist. Offer to say the words.)
4. Oil of catechumens: Priest anoints the person on the upper chest with oil of catechumens. A sign of strength.
5. Chrism: Priest anoints the person on the top of the head with chrism. A sign of joy. (Pass around to smell.)

Meditation:
   Invite children to think about these gifts, about the day of Baptism.
   Invite them to name the gifts.

Song:
- "The light of Christ has come into the world"
- "The light of Christ surrounds us . . . "
- "We are walking in the light"
- "I want to walk as a child of the light"

XI. **Work of the children**
   1. free drawings
   2. work with the material: pouring water over fist, saying words (During Easter Time keep some water in the font.)
   3. tracing packet
   4. collage work

CHAPTER SEVEN

The Atrium within the Parish

> It is the most profound adult formation program we have because we have so many adults involved.
> —a parishioner

The catechist in a parish is one who lives the Christian life, one who celebrates, grieves, does service, and prays with the local church. One of the great strengths of the Catechesis of the Good Shepherd is the catechist's in-depth training, which invites the adult not only to be with children in the atrium, but to embrace the whole life of the Church. Indeed, the life of the atrium is the life of the Church.

The many ministries of the parish surrounding the atrium are connected to it in numerous ways. Above all, the liturgical life of the Church gives rhythm and substance to the work and prayer of children. As the liturgical year unfolds, children change the cloths and candles in the atrium to the appropriate color. Even the presentations given to them are seasonal, and each age level's three-year curriculum can be matched to the Lectionary so that some of the prophecies, narratives, and parables heard on Sunday might also be pondered in the atrium. In the atrium children prepare for fuller and more conscious participation in the liturgy. They start to recognize words and gestures of the priest and assembly. They become able, through many repetitions of atrium "works," to prepare the cruets, wash the hands of the priest, and even dress the altar table. The communal prayer of the older ones is patterned on the Liturgy of the Hours. The children listen for and recognize themes familiar to them from the atrium in the hymns that are sung at the Eucharist. For example, the traditional Catholic hymn "Immaculate Mary" speaks of the Annunciation, the Visitation, the Birth of Jesus, the Crucifixion, and the Parousia.

The atrium, too, can impact the liturgy as children become more visible. They become equal listeners to the Word of God and may be invited to sit up close. Older ones can spread the light at the Easter Vigil. A parent and child might be chosen to take part in the preparation of the gifts. When an infant is baptized, children love to watch, standing or sitting near the font. In prayers or the homily, the presider might occasionally address God as Shepherd, the image that most resonates with the little ones.

Hymns can be chosen that reveal key moments of sacred history. The gestures of the priest, done slowly and intentionally for the children, draw everyone into the heart of the mystery.

There seems to be a natural bond between the Catechesis of the Good Shepherd and the RCIA. If a strong Christian initiation process exists in the parish, the groundwork is already laid for the atrium. There are many similarities between the two. Both are a kind of "de-schooled" religious formation in which the main textbook is the Bible. They both follow the liturgical year; the content of both atrium sessions and catechumenate sessions is seasonal. Some words are the same: *catechesis* and all its cognates, *atrium*, and so on. First Eucharist in the Catechesis of the Good Shepherd resembles initiation: It is a long process involving coming forward and writing one's name, receiving the Gospel, special meetings, prayers, the "handing over" and "return" of the Our Father, a retreat, a renewal of baptismal promises, and then the atrium child is clothed in the long white garment of initiation on First Communion day. In both the atrium and the RCIA, relationship is foundational—relationship with Christ and with the community.

At a board meeting of the National Association of the Catechesis of the Good Shepherd, a conversation revealed that many of the members present were involved in the ministry of Christian initiation as well as with the atrium. This has happened in many churches.

The deep and lengthy training of a catechist is always fruitful. Some catechists make a lifelong commitment to working with children; some also go on to train many other adults. Those who leave the atrium often embrace other parish ministries. Liturgy, in particular the proclamation of the Word, interests many catechists. Christian initiation and the pastoral care of the sick draw those who have served children to serve others at the edges of the community. Some catechists go on to take places on religious education boards or parish councils, bringing new perspectives on the priorities and values of the parish.

The method of the catechesis has also affected adults in their own occupations and in service to the poor. They have come to know that, when given the resources they need, people of all ages will take over their own education and work. "It has really changed my teaching," said one catechist who is a high school English teacher.

In some churches the atrium becomes a place of prayer and spiritual nourishment for groups of adults. Its very appropriate and historical use is by the catechumens after the Sunday dismissal. One catechist who serves the children in the parish school opens the atrium fifteen minutes before school begins so the teachers have a quiet place to gather for prayer and reflection on the readings of the day.

At first it may seem preferable for a new atrium to begin quietly and without much parish involvement. The catechists may not need much help, and if the atrium is unnoticed no one will ask questions about it. But much is lost if the atrium is hidden. The catechesis brings new learnings, growth, some criticism, the usual resistance to change, and often great healing. The youngest parishioners start to be heard through their drawings and prayers and comments that are observed and rejoiced in. If a catechist leader could be invited to join the religious education board or even the pastoral staff, this particular ministry to children would be more deeply connected to the whole of parish life.

The Catechesis of the Good Shepherd has been making links with the Church that go beyond local parishes. In the United States, while most atria are in Roman Catholic parishes, many churches that have opened an atrium are Episcopal; others are Lutheran, Presbyterian, or Methodist. There is a growing interest within the Orthodox tradition that is now seen around the country. Many of the catechists have developed a new interest in ecumenical issues. They find that they are brought together in formation courses by their shared response to the hunger for God in all children. Sectarian concerns move to the background, though the pain of eucharistic division continues.

Some catechists have read the 1982 document of the World Council of Churches, *Baptism, Eucharist, and Ministry*.[31] It seems that what most appeals to children about Baptism and Eucharist are the same aspects named in the document as common to the different Christian denominations. *Essentiality*, that is, the distillation of what is most basic and necessary, is a characteristic of the child. It is also a principle that has guided both the choice of subjects and the methodology in the catechesis. Essentiality also appears to be a force for unity among Christians.

Several things that could impede ecumenical progress are beginning to be overcome in the Good Shepherd Catechesis. In the past three decades there has been extensive dialogue among the churches at national and international levels, but often when some consensus is reached there, the reception among churches at the local level is minimal. The catechesis network is a community ready and eager to receive the concrete suggestions for church fellowship that result from ecumenical agreements.[32]

Sometimes ecumenism at the local level is dependent on chance events: the comings and goings of the local priest or rector, a parishioner with strong interests in ecumenism. The catechesis, though it is not really an institution, gives some stamina and security to ecumenical efforts and provides some grass-roots models.[33] There are several atriums in the United States, as well as one in Canada and one in Germany, that welcome children of different denominations.

The ecumenical aspect of the catechesis was a great surprise to everyone. Our different traditions, rather than being an obstacle, have made the Catechesis of the Good Shepherd even more appealing.

It seems that what leads us to move beyond boundaries is the unexpected. In 1995 and 1996 there were an alarming number of church fires, mostly in the southern part of the United States. One of the churches that burned to the ground housed an atrium that had been lovingly crafted by parishioners, the spiritual home of many children. Everything was lost: not only the church and all its records, but the painstaking work of many hands and the notes and albums of the catechists. With an outpouring of gifts, the atrium opened again in the school across the street, welcoming not only the parish children but those from a nearby homeless shelter.

The shape the catechesis will eventually take in a parish is unknown at the outset. Whom it will call, whom it will welcome, whom it will heal, how it will look and how slowly or rapidly it will evolve are yet to be discovered. "God, this is your work," is the prayer refrain of a catechist in a city church. Does the Catechesis of the Good Shepherd seem right for our parish? And if it is, is this the right time to begin? These are questions to be considered carefully. Because once children walk through the door of an atrium, something new has begun.

APPENDIX 1
Excerpts from a Catechist's Letter to Tina Lillig

February 24, 1997

May God's peace be with you! . . .

This catechesis has enriched the life of our parish at St. Anne's. We have a few more than five hundred children in five atria. Our program runs five days a week. About seventy-five of the children speak Spanish as their first language, so our atria are bilingual. Since only the written material needed to be adjusted we found it almost easy to make it bilingual, and this change brought many blessings to our community. . . .

Our pastor . . . is very supportive and has embraced this catechesis. At staff meetings I have presented many of the meditations and we have started to use these meditations to enhance the work of other ministries. For the preparation of parents desiring Baptism for their children, we have put the meditations for children age three to six together to form a single meditation which has been very beautiful. I love to watch for those fathers who come only because they love their wives. They start out so stern and unmoved and are often teary-eyed by the time they have received their light and have started to sing "This little light of mine." We also have used meditations for RCIA, on various retreats, and for ARISE (a program for returning Catholics). It was very moving to present the Found Sheep for these people who have been "lost" for a while. I also presented the Loving Father at our last reconciliation service.

This catechesis has changed my life and the life of my family. My children have never known a time when our family didn't serve the Lord, but we have never worked with more joy than we do now. My husband . . . has come to find he enjoys carpentry very much, since we make many of the materials together. My two teenage girls serve as aides and [daughter], age 8, has been in the atrium since she was 4. She is a constant source of wonder for me.

The children's sense of joy and peace is so contagious. I have never been more peaceful than when I am with the children. The first time I went on the

First Communion retreat, the peace and joy of the children was like a physical presence! To watch a child work in that state is at times more than I can bear; it is so beautiful. When I am giving a presentation, the children's peace can fill me and I know by experience rather than faith that we are on holy ground and the Lord is present. Every time I am privileged to see that silent conversation between creature and Creator I find I can love both God and the child even more. I used to say, "Thank you, Lord," but now I just say, "I love you."

It is amazing to me how beautiful the interrelationship between the atrium and the community is. So often at Mass I will see a small child explaining a gesture to their parents. We introduce the atrium to the children as a gift from the people of the parish and some time during the year they come to notice that almost everything is handmade. Our materials are made by many in the parish. All the supplies come from donations. (Each week the bulletin says, "The atrium will gladly accept donations of the following: triple-size cotton balls . . . ") It is at this moment, when a child asks, "Who made all this?" that the love of the community is illuminated for them. The community now has a way of showing the children that they are truly loved. Many anonymous gifts show up in the office. We have a bulletin board outside the atrium rooms to help educate the community to the work of the children. So often you will see adults standing silently for some time before their artwork or written prayer. I find myself doing it as well. One of these drawings is of the baby Jesus in a manger with Mary and Joseph, a cow and a lamb looking down at him. Almost a typical picture, except for the treasure box in the corner and the fact that this six-year-old drew this picture after hearing the parable of the hidden treasure for the first time. We, as a community, have come to see just a little of what Jesus meant when he told us to be like children to enter the Kingdom.

"Who is my neighbor?" Our children see that our neighbor may be in war-torn Bosnia, or in a poor part of inner-city Phoenix, or in the seat next to them. When the war was raging in Bosnia, Father . . . asked the community if anyone who worked in a hospital might have access to a portable suction pump—those are obsolete now, since hospitals have them built into the walls. That evening three showed up. The next day four more did, along with five boxes of assorted medical supplies. By the end of the week our narthex was filled with medical supplies, canned food, blankets, and clothes. By Christmas we had shipped five truckloads. Our children not only witnessed this but helped send soap, socks, and toys to the children there. When a poor church in

Phoenix had a fire, our community dug deep into their pockets, even though we were already trying to raise money to build our own church. When our deacon was diagnosed with pancreatic cancer, cards and letters filled with prayers and checks were sent not only to him but to his wife and five children as well. And when he died, it was the children who reminded us that he now shared fully in the Resurrection of Jesus. "See, Father is wearing white—it's a feast of joy." He died on his oldest daughter's thirteenth birthday and she decided that this was a good thing, that she would always celebrate her father's entrance into the Kingdom on the anniversary of her birth. We are blessed not with a rich parish, but with a generous one, rich in love. I think it helps our children see the abundance of our Lord's gifts. . . .

In God's love, peace and joy,
Mary Mirrione
Catechesis of the Good Shepherd Coordinator
Atrium of the Little Flower at Saint Anne's

APPENDIX 2
The Characteristics of the Catechesis of the Good Shepherd: Thirty-Two Points of Reflection

What are the principal points which distinguish this catechesis and because of which it is called the "Catechesis of the Good Shepherd"? The following characteristics are intended to represent the principal aspects of the catechesis as they have emerged after more than sixty years of work with children of different countries, cultures, and socioeconomic backgrounds. These characteristics are reflective of the constants which have presented themselves in this work and are presented here with the invitation to go deeper into them for further reflection.

1. The child, particularly the religious life of the child, is central to the interest and commitment of the catechist of the Good Shepherd.

    The catechist observes and studies the vital needs of the child and the manifestations of those vital needs according to the developmental stage of the child.

    The catechists live with the child a shared religious experience according to the teaching of the Gospel: "Except you become like little children, you cannot enter the kingdom of God" (Matthew 18:3).

    The catechist attends to the conditions which are necessary for this life to be experienced and to flourish.

2. With this aim in mind, the catechist embraces Maria Montessori's vision of the human being, and thus the attitude of the adult regarding the child; and prepares an environment called the atrium, which aids the development of the religious life.

3. The atrium is a community in which children and adults live together a religious experience that facilitates participation in the wider community of the family, the church, and other social spheres.

The atrium is a place of prayer, in which work and study spontaneously become meditation, contemplation, and prayer.

The atrium is a place in which the only Teacher is Christ; both children and adults place themselves in a listening stance before his Word and seek to penetrate the mystery of the liturgical celebration.

4. The transmission of the Christian message in the atrium has a celebrative character.

    The catechist is not a teacher, remembering that the only Teacher is Christ himself.

    The catechist renounces every form of control (such as quizzes, texts, exams, etc.) in the spirit of poverty before an experience whose fruits are not her or his own.

5. The themes presented in the atrium are those to which the children have responded with depth and joy. These themes are taken from the Bible and the liturgy (prayers and sacraments) as the fundamental sources for creating and sustaining Christian life at every developmental stage and, in particular, for illuminating and nourishing the child in his or her most vital religious needs.

6. The Word is proclaimed in the most objective manner possible so that the words of the adult do not impede the communication between God, who speaks, and God's creature, who listens. The only aim of the words of the adult is to discreetly serve the listening to God's Word, in accordance with Jesus' own statement in the Gospel: "My teaching is not mine but his who sent me" (John 7:16).

7. The catechist of the Good Shepherd does not incorporate into the catechesis themes other than those which emerge from the essentiality and specificity of the vital needs of the children and our work with them.

8. The weekly atrium gatherings should last at least two hours, of which a small part is often dedicated to the catechist's presentation, and the majority of the time is reserved for the personal work of the child.

9. In harmony with the universal Church, the life in the atrium follows the liturgical year; therefore, moments which are particularly intense are those of Christmas/Epiphany and Easter/Pentecost.

10. Eucharist is central to the life of the atrium at every level, according to the various denominations of the Christian church in which the atrium is located.

11. At the annual announcement of the celebration of First Communion, the children respond according to the desire for the sacrament and their personal maturity, which is discerned with the help of the family, the catechists and the priest.

12. The celebration of First Communion is preceded by an intense period of preparation consisting of special weekly gatherings other than the regular atrium sessions.

13. The retreat for First Communion lasts at least four days (from morning to evening). Essential elements of the retreat include:
    - a daily celebration of Eucharist;
    - sufficient opportunity for the children to work in peace with what they have already been given without receiving new presentations;
    - extension of the retreat until the evening also on the day of First Communion so that the children are not too quickly distracted from what they have lived.

14. The celebration of first Reconciliation is solemnly linked to the baptismal signs of the white garment and the light, and, in the case of catechumens, of the celebration of Baptism.

15. The attention given to meetings with families intensifies during the period leading up to First Communion.

16. The catechesis continues in the years which follow First Communion, returning to and enlarging upon themes already introduced and presenting other themes according to the new needs of the emerging developmental period.

17. A material is placed at the disposal of the children. The children's personal work with the material aids their meditation on and absorption of the theme presented. In settings where it is not possible to have an atrium yet, another valid instrument for announcing the Christian message consists of the workbooks and catechists' guidebooks: "I Am the Good Shepherd." The voice of the Good Shepherd can reach the child through different instruments, but regardless of the particular instrument, the voice of the Shepherd resounds in the depths of the heart.

18. The material must be attractive but "sober" and must strictly adhere to the theme being presented. In making the material, the catechist refrains from adding superficial embellishments that would distract the child from the essentials of the theme being presented. In other words, the material must be simple, essential, and "poor" in order to allow the richness of the themes' content to shine through.

19. This same guideline (as in #18) applies to the atrium environment itself. The Catechesis of the Good Shepherd can be realized in any social or cultural setting.

20. The materials prepared by catechists for the atrium are faithful to the experimental models of the Catechesis of the Good Shepherd. The designs of these models are the result of a long, collaborative work of observation and experimentation and have been developed according to the needs of the child at each developmental stage.

21. The material makes it possible for the catechist to assume his or her proper "post" as "the useless servant" (Luke 17:10). This expression indicates that the catechist has a task to perform, a role to fulfill, whose results, however, go much farther from what he or she does, because the only Teacher is Christ.

22. The catechists work together in a spirit of unity and harmony, in tune with God's plan for communion in the history of salvation and in keeping with the themes of unity so strongly expressed in the parables of the Good Shepherd (John 10:1ff.) and the True Vine (John 15:1ff.). They generously offer their talents and experience for the good of all.

23. The attitude of the adult has to be marked by humility before the capacities of the child, establishing a right rapport with the child—that is to say, respecting the personality of the child and waiting for the child to reveal himself or herself.

24. The tasks of the catechist include

    going deeper into the Christian message through the knowledge of the biblical and liturgical sources and of ongoing living tradition of the Church, including the theological, social, and ecumenical movements which enliven the Church today;

    preparing an environment and maintaining order in that environment (the atrium) so that it fosters concentration, silence, and contemplation in both the child and adult; and

    preparing the materials oneself as much as possible while collaborating with others in areas that are beyond one's abilities.

25. The reasons why the catechist is requested to make the materials with his or her own hands are

    to absorb the content more deeply;

    to combat hurry, consumerism, and even excessive "efficiency";

    to pace oneself more to the rhythm of the child and thus also—or so we believe—to the working of the Holy Spirit; and

    to try to reach the integration of hand, mind, and heart.

26. The primary commitment of the catechist is working with the children in the atrium; however, this commitment also leads the catechist to be open to the needs of the catechesis in general and makes him or her responsive to other forms of service that might be necessary.

27. The Catechesis of the Good Shepherd is also concerned with helping adults open their eyes to the hidden riches of the child, especially to the child's spiritual wealth, so that adults will be drawn to learn from the child and to serve him or her. The guiding principles in this endeavor are the following:

The Catechesis of the Good Shepherd does not seek success.

It does not set about to be important or to impress others (Isaiah 10:33–11:10).

It is faithful to the spirit of the mustard seed (Matthew 13:31).

It stands in solidarity with the least in the Church.

28. The Catechesis of the Good Shepherd especially honors the spiritual values of childhood and wishes to nurture the formation of a consciousness which is oriented to the construction of the history of salvation in justice and solidarity.

29. The Catechesis of the Good Shepherd is open to all Christians of various denominations and of different commitments within the Church.

30. The Catechesis of the Good Shepherd offers its services to the diocese and therefore works in communion with the bishop.

31. Every atrium avails itself of the help of a priest who is attentive to the children, particularly to their religious capacities, celebrates Eucharist and the Sacrament of Reconciliation with them, and works in harmony with the spirit of the Catechesis of the Good Shepherd.

32. The Catechesis of the Good Shepherd has an experimental character and is open to go always deeper into the infinite mystery of God and God's cosmic covenant with God's creatures.

NOTES

Chapter 1

1. Sofia Cavalletti, *The Religious Potential of the Child* (Chicago: Liturgy Training Publications, 1992).

2. Cavalletti, *The Religious Potential of the Child*, 22.

3. The following biographical information is taken from two sources: a lecture given by Cavalletti in Toronto in July 1986, and Jerome W. Berryman, "Montessori Religious Education: Sofia Cavalletti (1917–2011)," PACE (May 1994): 3–7.

4. E. M. Standing, ed., *The Child in the Church* (St. Paul, MN: Catechetical Guild Education Society, 1965).

5. There is a similar resource for children ages six to nine—a wooden "Bible" which opens to reveal blocks of wood that represent each book, in sizes corresponding to the length of the actual book. There are accompanying charts to help the child group the books according to their order and genre, and a booklet entitled "What Is the Bible?"

6. Cavalletti, *The Religious Potential of the Child*, 65–66.

7. The image of Christ as shepherd was also the choice of the first Christians, as may be seen in the catacombs. It was the most prevalent of all the symbolic representations of Christ.

Chapter 2

1. Patricia Coulter, "Adults in Ministry with Children" (DMIN thesis proposal, Toronto School of Theology, rev. April 20, 1995), 2.

2. Gabe Huck, ed., *A Common Sense for Parish Life* (Chicago: Liturgy Training Publications, 1995), 18.

3. Barbara Schmich, "The Catechesis of the Good Shepherd," *Liturgy*, Fall 1989, 74.

4. This thought was expressed in a letter from Halleta Heinrich, July 16, 1994.

5. Sofia Cavalletti, Patricia Coulter, Gianna Gobbi and Silvana Q. Montanaro, *The Good Shepherd and the Child: A Joyful Journey* (New Rochelle, NY: Don Bosco Multimedia, 1994).

6. The Catechesis of the Good Shepherd, 7655 East Main Street, Scottsdale, AZ, 480-874-3759.

7. The following information on levels of formation, content of courses, and course formats was organized by Elizabeth Hissong.

8. Costs will be discussed in more detail in chapter 3.

9. See Barbara Schmich, "The Formation of Children," *Assembly*, June 1987, 374–376; Carol Dittberner, "The Pure Wonder of Young Lives," *Sojourners*, January 1987, 21–25; Schmich, "The Catechesis of the Good Shepherd," *Liturgy*, Fall 1989, 73–78; Robert R. Holton, "Holy Things," *Our Sunday Visitor*, April 14, 1996, 12–13; Barbara Matera, "The Catechesis of the Good Shepherd: A Way of Experiencing God," *Pastoral Liturgy* 43, no. 3 (May/June 2012): 4–9.

Chapter 3

1. These thoughts on the value of making materials are found in an article by Gianna Gobbi, "Letters from Sofia and Gianna," published in the 1996–1997 *Journal*. This is available in the compilation *Journals of the Catechesis of the Good Shepherd: 1984–1997* (Chicago: Liturgy Training Publications, 1998), 282–283.

2. "Catechesis of the Good Shepherd: Points of Reflection," 16, document prepared for discussion at the October 1993 international meeting in Rome.

3. Maria Christlieb, "The Catechesis of the Good Shepherd in Chihuahua, Northern Mexico," *Journal*, Winter 1984, compiled in *Journals of the Catechesis of the Good Shepherd: 1984–1997* (Chicago: Liturgy Training Publications, 1998), 9–10.

4. Carol Dittberner, "The Seed Grows," *Journal*, Winter 1984, compiled in *Journals of the Catechesis of the Good Shepherd: 1984–1997* (Chicago: Liturgy Training Publications, 1998), 20–21.

5. See examples at the end of this chapter.

Chapter 4

1. Betsy Puntel, "'Atrium'–The 'Where' of Catechesis," *The Living Light*, Summer 1990, 351.

2. A beautiful example is the church of Santa Maria in Trastevere, Rome, Italy.

3. Standing, *The Child in the Church*, 35.

4. Cavalletti, *The Religious Potential of the Child*, 56.

Chapter 5

1. Dieter Seiler, "*Fides Infantium:* A Conversion," *Concilium*, 1996, no. 2, 68.

Chapter 6

1. Anton A. Bucher, "Children as Subjects," *Concilium*, 1996, no. 2.

2. Bucher, "Children as Subjects," 46.

3. The shift to an initiation vocabulary was clarified by Jeanette Lucinio in her 1994 Summer Institute course, "The Best Kept Secret," at Catholic Theological Union, Chicago.

4. See example of an album page at the end of this chapter.

Chapter 7

1. World Council of Churches, *Baptism, Eucharist and Ministry* (Geneva: World Council of Churches, 1982).

2. Institute for Ecumenical Research, *Crisis and Challenge of the Ecumenical Movement* (Geneva: World Council of Churches, 1994), 10–11.

3. Institute for Ecumenical Research, 21.

BIBLIOGRAPHY

Berryman, Jerome W. "Montessori Religious Education: Sofia Cavalletti (1917–2011)." *PACE*, May 1994, 3–7.

Bucher, Anton A. "Children as Subjects." *Concilium* 1996, no. 2, 43–52.

"Catechesis of the Good Shepherd: Points of Reflection." October 1993 International Meeting, Rome, Italy. (Mimeographed.)

Cavalletti, Sofia. *The Religious Potential of the Child*. Chicago: Liturgy Training Publications, 1992.

Cavalletti, Sofia, Patricia Coulter, Gianna Gobbi, Silvana Q. Montanaro, and Rebekah Rojcewicz. *The Good Shepherd and the Child: A Joyful Journey*. New Rochelle, New York: Don Bosco Multimedia, 1994.

Christlieb, Maria. "The Catechesis of the Good Shepherd in Chihuahua, Northern Mexico." *Journals of the Catechesis of the Good Shepherd: 1984–1997*. Chicago: Liturgy Training Publications, 1998, 9–10.

Coulter, Patricia. "Adults in Ministry with Children: Catechesis of the Good Shepherd." DMIN thesis proposal, Toronto School of Theology, revised 1995.

Dittberner, Carol. "The Pure Wonder of Young Lives." *Sojourners*, January 1987, 21–25.

———. "The Seed Grows." *Journals of the Catechesis of the Good Shepherd: 1984–1997*. Chicago: Liturgy Training Publications, 1998, 20–21.

Holton, Robert R. "Holy Things." *Our Sunday Visitor*, April 14, 1996, 12–13.

Huck, Gabe, ed. *A Common Sense for Parish Life*. Chicago: Liturgy Training Publications, 1995.

Institute for Ecumenical Research. *Crisis and Challenge of the Ecumenical Movement*. Geneva: World Council of Churches, 1994.

Puntel, Betsy. "'Atrium'—The 'Where' of Catechesis." *The Living Light* 26, no. 4 (Summer 1990): 348–352.

Schmich, Barbara. "The Catechesis of the Good Shepherd." *Liturgy* 8, no. 2 (Fall 1989): 73–79.

———. "The Formation of Children." *Assembly*, June 1987, 374–376.

Seiler, Dieter. "*Fides Infantium:* A Conversion." *Concilium*, 1996, no. 2, 64–75.

Standing, E. M., ed., *The Child in the Church.* St. Paul, Minnesota: Catechetical Guild Education Society, 1965.

World Council of Churches. *Baptism, Eucharist and Ministry.* Geneva: World Council of Churches, 1982.

ADDITIONAL CATECHESIS OF THE GOOD SHEPHERD PUBLICATIONS

A Is for Altar, B Is for Bible
   Judith Lang Main

A Year with Sofia Cavalletti: The Theological and Spiritual Influences of the Catechesis of the Good Shepherd
   Ann Garrido

The Journals of the Catechesis of the Good Shepherd, 1984–present.

Living in Joyful Hope: Advent and Christmas Meditations
   Suzanne M. Lewis

Mustard Seed Preaching
   Ann Garrido

The Development of the Catechesis of the Good Shepherd: Inside the Atrium in Rome
   Sofia Cavalletti

The Religious Potential of the Child
   Sofia Cavalletti

The Religious Potential of the Child, 6 to 12 Years Old
   Sofia Cavalletti

Ways to Nurture the Relationship with God
   Sofia Cavalletti and Patricia Coulter

Buen Pastor y el niño
   Sofia Cavalletti, Patricia Coulter, Gianna Gobbi, and Silvana Q. Montanarop, **MD**

El potencial religioso del niño
   Sofia Cavalletti

Catechesis of the Good Shepherd Publications is an imprint of Liturgy Training Publications (LTP).

Further information about these publications is available from LTP or from: The Catechesis of the Good Shepherd, 7655 East Main Street, Scottsdale, AZ 85251; phone 408-874-3757; email cgs@cgsusa.org. Requests for information about other aspects of the Catechesis should be directed to this address.

More information about the method of the Catechesis and locations of atria and adult formation courses can be found on the CGSUSA website: www.cgsusa.org.